# A RIVER JOURNEY

# *The* **Rhine**

### Ronan Foley

943.4
Foley

# A RIVER JOURNEY

| The Amazon | The Ganges |
|---|---|
| The Mississippi | The Nile |
| The Rhine | The Yangtze |

*A River Journey: The Rhine*

Text copyright © 2004 Raintree
Series copyright © 2004 Raintree
Published by Raintree, a division of Reed Elsevier, Inc..

Copyright Permissions
Raintree
100 N. Lasalle, Suite 1200
Chicago, IL 60602

Book design: Jane Hawkins
Picture Research: Shelley Noronha, Glass Onion Pictures
Researchers: Simon Milligan & Martin Curtis
Maps: Tony Fleetwood

**Library of Congress Cataloging-in-Publication Data:**

Cataloging-in-publication data is on file at the Library of Congress.

ISBN 0-7398-6073-9

Printed in Hong Kong.
1 2 3 4 5 6 7 8 9 0
08 07 06 05 04

The website addresses (URLs) included in this
book were valid at the time of going to press.
However, because of the nature of the Internet, it is
possible that some addresses may have changed,
or sites may have changed or closed down since
publication. While the author and Publisher regret
any inconvenience this may cause readers,
no responsibility for any such changes can be
accepted by either the author or the Publisher.

The maps in this book use a conical projection,
and so the indictor for North on the main map
is only approximate.

**Picture Acknowledgments**
Cover: Bob Krist/Corbis; title page: Eye Ubiquitous; 3 Hodder Wayland Picture Library; 5 Skyscan; 6 Hugh
Rooney/Eye Ubiquitous; 7 (left) David Cumming/Eye Ubiquitous (right) Richard Wagner/AKG Photo; 8 Bernd
Ducke/Britstock-Ifa; 9 Eye Ubiquitous; 10 Skyscan; 11 (left) Topham, (right) Neil Egerton/Travel Ink, (bottom)
Ray Roberts/Impact; 12 Skyscan; 13 James Davis; 14 Topham; 15 Bryan Pickering/Eye Ubiquitous; 16 Peter
Siegenthaler/Britstock-Ifa; 17 Skyscan; 18 (left & right) Skyscan, 19 (left) Christophe Bluntzer/Impact, (right)
James Davis; 19 (bottom) Jim McDonald/Corbis; 20 Popperfoto/Reuters; 21 (left) Skyscan, (right) Gerard
Lacounette/Bios; 22 (left) Skyscan 4870, 22/23 (top) Gerard Lacounette/Bios; 23 Skyscan; 24 Stephen
Coyne/Ecoscene; 24/25 James Davis; 26 Denis Bringard/Bios; 27 Bernd Ducke/Britstock-Ifa; 27 (bottom) Nick
Weiseman/Eye Ubiquitous/Corbis; 28 Sally Morgan/Ecoscene; 29 David Cumming/Eye Ubiquitous; 30 Topham;
31 Bryan Pickering/Eye Ubiquitous, (top right) G. Graefenhain/Britstock-Ifa; 32 Robert Harding; 33
Popperfoto/Reuters; 34 Sally Morgan/Ecoscene; 35 Hodder Wayland Picture Library; 36 (top)
Schmidbauer/Britstock-Ifa, (bottom) Skyscan; 37 Skyscan, (bottom right) Hodder Wayland Picture Library; 38
Robert Harding; 39 Geospace/Science Photo Library; 40 (left) Graham Kitching/Ecoscene; 40/41 Peter
Palmer/Eye Ubiquitous; 41 (right) Larry Lee Photography/Corbis; 42 Mark Edwards/Still Pictures; 43 Robert
Harding; 44 Mark Edwards/Still Pictures; 45 Anthony Cooper/Ecoscene

# Contents

NORTH SEA

**MOUTH**

**5**

*Ijsselmeer*

Amsterdam

Ijssel River

NETHERLANDS

Lek River

Rotterdam          Arnhem

Ruhr River

BELGIUM          Cologne          Sieg River          GERMANY

BONN

Lahn River

Koblenz

Moselle River          Frankfurt

**4**

Main River

LUXEMBOURG          Mainz

**3**

Neckar River

Strasbourg

Black Forest

FRANCE

**2**

Rhine River          Constance          *Lake Constance*          **1**

Basel          Bregenz

LIECHTENSTEIN

AUSTRIA

**SOURCE**          Chur          Klosters

Reichenau

SWITZERLAND          Vorderrhein          Hinterrhein          Alps

ITALY

drainage basin          mountain ranges

N

miles  0          25          50          75

kilometers  0          50          100

# Your Guide to the River

**USING THEMED TEXT** As you make your journey down the Rhine you will find topic headings about that area of the river. These symbols show what the text is about.

**NATURE** Plants, wildlife, and the environment

**HISTORY** Events and people in the past

**PEOPLE** The lives and culture of local people

**CHANGE** Things that have altered the area

**$ ECONOMY** Jobs and industry in the area

**USING MAP REFERENCES** Each chapter has a map that shows the section of the river we are visiting. The numbered boxes show exactly where a place of interest is located.

# The Journey Ahead

The Rhine begins as a stream from a lake high in the Swiss Alps. On its journey it crosses six countries and travels 820 miles (1,320 kilometers) to the North Sea. After thundering down mountainsides in Switzerland, the Rhine levels off as it flows through the tiny country of Liechtenstein. It then forms the border between Switzerland and Austria until it reaches the beautiful Lake Constance. It goes on to wind its way to Basel from Lake Constance, forming the Swiss-German border in places.

The Rhine then heads toward the German cities of Mannheim and Mainz, where it again forms a border, this time between France and Germany. At Mainz, the river loops around again and heads into the classic Rhine countryside of steep-sided valleys, vineyards, and castles. After flowing past the German city of Cologne, the river flows through the great industrial area of the Ruhr at Duisburg. When the Rhine crosses into the Netherlands, it splits into several channels. The channels join together as the river completes its course near the great port and city of Rotterdam.

We start our river journey with a flight over the Swiss Alps and the source of the Rhine.

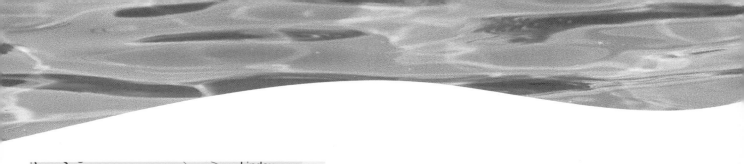

# 1. *The Alpine Rhine*

OUR JOURNEY BEGINS WITH A FLIGHT over the Rhine from its source in Switzerland's mountains to the point at which it flows into Lake Constance. The turbulent river hurtles through the mountainous landscape below us. Natural hazards such as floods and landslides are common in this region. As the landscape flattens, the Rhine levels out and becomes slightly more calm, but the river is still a powerful force. We see the first attempts to control the Rhine between the small country of Liechtenstein and Lake Constance, where we land and board a boat.

Below: The snowcapped Alps mark the beginning of the Rhine's long journey to the sea.

Above: In this poster for Wagner's opera about Rhinegold, a dwarf steals gold from the bed of the river. Left: The Rhine begins life as a trickling stream from the waters of Lake Tuma.

## NATURE *Source of the Rhine*

Most people consider Lake Tuma to be the source of the Rhine, but some geographers claim there is an alternative source. They believe it is a tributary called the *Hinterrhein* (meaning "back Rhine"), which begins life from the meltwaters of the Rheinwaldhorn Glacier MAP REF: 1 . The glacier is the starting point for the many streams and rivers that flow into the Rhine. But we will treat Lake Tuma as the start of our journey.

At a height of 7,694 feet (2,345 meters), Lake Tuma is located in a valley carved out by glaciers during the last Ice Age, which happened more than 10,000 years ago. The steep, mountainous walls rising around the lake are called cirques. The stream leaving Lake Tuma is at this point known as *Vorderrhein,* which means "front Rhine."

## HISTORY *The Rhinegold legend*

The headwaters of the Rhine are cloaked in history and legend. The most famous is a German legend about gold. The story tells of an enormous amount of gold hidden in the mountains near the Rhine that is fiercely guarded by the mountain people who live there. In 1869 the German composer Wagner used this legend as the inspiration for one of his famous operas.

Gold and many other metals have been found in the Alps near the Rhine and are still found today. Gold was always the most important, because it was used to make coins until the early 18th century.

The alpenhorn is a musical instrument unique to Switzerland. Farmers originally used the alpenhorn to call cows back into their pasture.

 **NATURE** *Mountain habitats*

The mountainous landscape of Switzerland is covered with snow and ice between November and March each year. Only the hardiest of animals can survive such harsh conditions. One animal is the chamois (pronounced sham-EE), a mountain goat. People used to produce an extremely soft leather from the skin of the chamois. Now it is a protected species.

As temperatures rise in the spring, the mountains come to life. Alpine plants appear, such as edelweiss, the Swiss national flower. The few farmers who live in this region have goats and sheep that graze on the fresh mountain pastures.

 **PEOPLE** *Swiss languages*

The two mountain channels, the Vorderrhein and the Hinterrhein, meet at Reichenau, Germany, near the Swiss city of Chur. From this point the river is known simply as the Rhine. By the time we reach Reichenau, the Rhine has already fallen over a third of its total descent to sea level from its source. The river flows through Switzerland and then north, toward the tiny, but wealthy, country of Liechtenstein.

Switzerland is famous for its watches, chocolate, and cheese, but it is also known for the four languages that are spoken there. Three of the languages—French, German, and Italian—are shared with neighbors. The fourth language, Romansch, is uniquely Swiss. Romansch is spoken by about 50,000 people, who live mainly in Graubünden region in the Rhine valley. Romansch is a mixture of Latin and Old French. Some words might sound familiar, such as *bun di*, which means "good day," or *cuppina,* which means "cup."

## $ ECONOMY *Liechtenstein's industry*

As we fly over Liechtenstein, the Rhine starts to flatten and flow more slowly. Liechtenstein is only 62 square miles (160 square kilometers) in size—one seventh the size of the state of Rhode Island. It has a population of just 32,500 people, which makes it one of the smallest countries in the world.

The Rhine is important to Liechtenstein because it forms the country's border with Switzerland to the west. Its capital, Vaduz MAP REF: 2 , sits on the eastern bank of the river, guarded by an impressive castle that was built in the 14th century.

Today, Liechtenstein is an important economic center. The country and its residents are wealthy. Banking is a major industry, employing about 15 percent of the workforce. Liechtenstein also has a large dental industry. There are many highly skilled dentists and dental technicians employed there. The country is the world's biggest exporter of dentures.

The capital of Liechtenstein, Vaduz, is overlooked by an impressive castle.

### ➡ CHANGE *Taming the Rhine*

Small dams have been built across the Rhine to cope with the seasonal changes in the river's water flow. Every year, the spring meltwaters surge down the steep-sided valleys, carrying soil and rocks downstream. The dams, some of which are large metal nets, are designed to catch this debris and prevent it from damaging towns and villages further downstream. As the Rhine widens and slows, it begins to naturally deposit its rocks in and alongside the river.

From Liechtenstein onward, flooding used to cause huge problems because the land was quite flat. For hundreds of years, the Rhine frequently would burst its banks during the spring. To protect residents and valuable farmland from the floods, the river was "channelized" in the early 19th century. When a river is channelized, it is forced to flow between raised embankments instead of flooding onto the surrounding land. But rivers are a powerful force. Some geographers believe that a river will resist such change over time and will try to return to its natural course. If the Rhine were to burst its artificial embankments, water would surge onto the surrounding land very rapidly.

Below: This channel in Liechtenstein controls and straightens the course of the river. The stones reinforce the riverbanks.

Above: The Cresta Run is a famous bobsled course.
Left: Davos, in Switzerland, is one of many winter resorts that attracts thousands of tourists.

## 👋 PEOPLE *Mountain livelihoods*

Traditional mountain livelihoods are rapidly disappearing. People used to make their living from farming and hunting wild animals. Today, people are finding new ways to earn their livings.

Tourism is the most important source of income in the mountain regions of Grabubünden and Ticino. In the summer the mountains are popular with walkers and climbers, but winter sports like skiing and snow-boarding attract the most visitors.

Some of the ski resorts, such as Davos and Klosters, are world famous. They are located on tributaries of the Rhine. There is also a well-known bobsled course, known as the Cresta Run, near the town of St. Moritz.

Tourism in Switzerland employs about 350,000 people, though many of these jobs are seasonal. In the Alpine Rhine region, where skiing accounts for about 70 percent of tourism, local people may have several jobs throughout the year. They work as ski instructors during the winter and as mountain guides during the summer. In the fall they take time off or help prepare the resorts for the next season.

After landing, we transfer to a lake steamer to continue our journey across the beautiful Lake Constance.

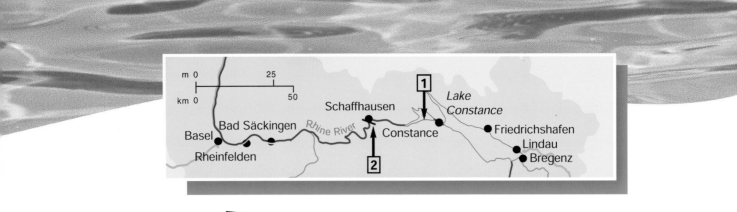

Schaffhausen

Rhine River

Constance

Lake Constance

1

2

Friedrichshafen

Lindau

Bregenz

Basel

Bad Säckingen

Rheinfelden

# 2. The Upper Rhine

AFTER CROSSING LAKE CONSTANCE, we board a smaller boat that will take us to the spectacular Falls of the Rhine. Below the falls, we return to the river, which is now safe for boats to navigate for the rest of its course. From Rheinfelden, we begin to see the importance of the Rhine for commercial river traffic. By the time we reach Basel in Switzerland we have descended an additional 492 feet (150 meters) through the slow meanders of the Rhine that form the border between Switzerland and Germany.

Below: The muddy Rhine tumbles into the light blue water of Lake Constance near the town of Bregenz.

Right: The walled town of Lindau is a popular tourist destination. This tourist cruise boat is about to explore Lake Constance.

### 🐰 NATURE  *River to lake*

The Rhine enters Lake Constance near Bregenz in a rather unusual way, which is easier to see from the air than from land. The muddy river tumbles into the clear blue lake in a long stream of water, like a short canal. The effect looks like an underwater waterfall. This happens because the turbulent river sediment meets the calm lake water. This feature is known locally as the *Rheinbrech.* The Rhine essentially sinks below and runs under the surface of the lake, emerging again as a river 40 miles (65 kilometers) to the west to continue its journey downstream.

### 💲 ECONOMY  *Lake Constance & tourism*

Lake Constance is the largest lake in Germany, even though it is shared with Switzerland and Austria. Known to German speakers as Bodensee, Lake Constance is surrounded by rolling hills and picturesque towns, particularly on the German side of the lake. It is very popular with tourists, and the tourist industry there supports hundreds of jobs. More than 170,000 tourists each year visit the city of Constance, and at least 80 percent of them come from within Germany itself.

Constance, the city, actually stretches across the German border into Switzerland and is therefore a city in two countries.

Many tourists take a boat trip on the lake, and they also come to visit the local towns and cities. The walled town of Lindau is of special interest. It stands on an island connected to the mainland by a bridge and a causeway.

Our steamer stops at Reichenau Island MAP REF: 1 , where we visit St. George's Church, one of the lake's most popular attractions. The church is famous for its frescoes, or wall paintings, that date back as far as the 9th century. The sights of Lake Constance are beautiful, and many people come here just to enjoy the clean mountain air, particularly during the warm and bright summers.

*The Zeppelins*

On the northern shore of Lake Constance is Friedrichshafen, a town famous as the home of giant airships known as zeppelins. A German nobleman, Ferdinand Graf von Zeppelin, invented these enormous airships. The first flight of a zeppelin, the LZ1, took place over Lake Constance on July 2, 1900. A total of 119 zeppelins, each the length of two soccer fields, were built in Friedrichshafen between 1900 and 1938.

During World War I, Germans used Zeppelins to drop bombs. After the war they were used mainly for luxury air travel. In 1929, the airship *Graf Zeppelin* (also known as LZ127) left Lake Constance to fly around the world, stopping in New York, Tokyo, and Los Angeles before returning to the lake.

In May 1937, a zeppelin named the *Hindenburg,* which had successfully flown across the Atlantic Ocean 21 times, caught fire as it came in to land at Lakehurst, New Jersey. The zeppelin caught fire because the silver paint used on it was highly flammable. The zeppelin was filled with hydrogen gas which, combined with an electrical discharge from the silver paint, caused the airship to rapidly catch fire. Only 12 passengers are known to have survived. Because of passengers' fears following this disaster, zeppelins were no longer built.

In 2000, however, a zeppelin built with new technology was successfully launched in Friedrichshafen to celebrate the zeppelin's 100th birthday.

The first zeppelin makes its maiden voyage over Lake Constance in July 1900.

 **NATURE** *The Falls of the Rhine*

About 12 miles (20 kilometers) after leaving Lake Constance, the Rhine meets a major obstacle—the Falls of the Rhine MAP REF: 2 at Schaffhausen. The river suddenly speeds up as it is forced through a 492-foot- (150-meter-) wide gorge before plunging vertically for 76 feet (23 meters) as a thundering, foaming mass of white water. The Falls of the Rhine are a popular tourist site. They attracted more than 1.5 million visitors in 2000.

Depending on the time of year, between 24,700 and 38,200 cubic feet (700 to 1,080 cubic meters) of water plunge over the falls every second. That is equivalent to filling

Above: Tourists get a closer look at the Falls of the Rhine from the viewing station at the right of the photograph.

about 20 Olympic-sized swimming pools every minute. The falls reach their peak flow during the spring, when the mountain snow melts and swells the river system.

Waterfalls are normally found where rivers meet hard rocks—in this case limestone—that are difficult to erode. As the softer rock downstream continues to erode, the riverbed falls away and creates a sudden drop in the river. This process usually takes many thousands of years. Geologists believe that the Falls of the Rhine were formed about 15,000 years ago.

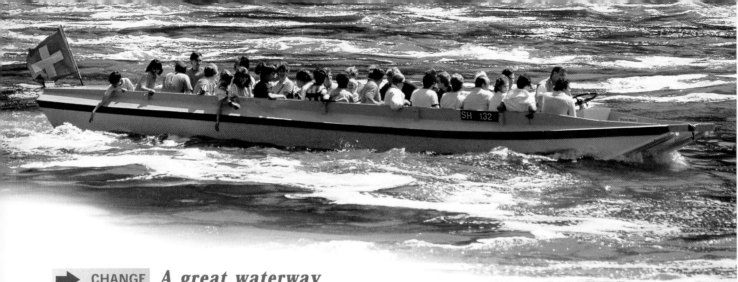

## ➡️ CHANGE  *A great waterway*

The Rhine carries more river traffic than any other waterway in the world. In 2001, an estimated 220 million tons of cargo were transported on the river, which is equivalent to the amount carried by 366,000 trucks! This is twice as much cargo as is carried on the Seine River in France and almost four times as much as on the Danube River of Central Europe.

Despite its importance as a waterway, the Rhine is not navigable by boat until the town of Rheinfelden, about 31 miles (50 kilometers) downstream of the Falls of the Rhine. This is because the higher Rhine is too dangerous for boats. Between the Falls of the Rhine and Rheinfelden, the river is blocked by a series of dams. Originally, planners had hoped to make the Rhine navigable upstream as far as Constance. This was never achieved, but river journeys on the Rhine are still measured from Constance. This means that our boat journey starts 93 miles (149 kilometers) further west at Rheinfelden.

As part of a network of European waterways, the Rhine is now joined to the Danube River by a canal near Nürnberg. The

> The best way to explore the Rhine is by boat. This large speedboat carries tourists down the river.

Rhine-Main-Danube Canal was completed in 1992. It is an important trade route for ships sailing between the Atlantic Ocean and the Black Sea.

## 💲 ECONOMY  *Powering the way*

At the turn of the 20th century, European scientists were experimenting with methods of generating electricity. One of their challenges was to find out how to capture the enormous power needed to turn the generators to create electricity. They soon turned to the Rhine for their answer. The fast-flowing water provided a constant and free source of power that could be used to turn the generators as it flowed downstream. This hydroelectric power (HEP) was first developed at Rheinfelden in 1898, with the building of Europe's first HEP plant. Other power stations have since been built on many of the fast-flowing tributaries that tumble down from the Alps and the mountains surrounding the

Black Forest. The tributaries are ideal for generating HEP. Even though they are small, their steep gradient gives the water greater power.

 **NATURE** *Water into energy*

The water needed to generate HEP is normally stored behind a dam across a valley. It is then released to power the generators. Storing the water in this way has the added benefit of controlling flooding because water can be released slowly over time.

HEP is also beneficial for the environment because it produces electricity without the harmful emissions of other methods, such as coal or gas-fired power stations. Because global warming is a concern for everyone, clean forms of energy such as HEP are increasingly important.

Below: The hydroelectric plant at the bottom left of the photograph is more than 100 years old. It was the first of its type to be built in Europe.

## 📖 HISTORY *Historic towns & abbeys*

We pass a number of historic sites along the peaceful Rhine River between Schaffhausen and Basel. At Rheinau a Benedictine abbey built in 1705 juts into the river on a small peninsula of land that is actually in Switzerland. Thirty-one miles (50 kilometers) downstream of Rheinfelden, we pass under a bridge in the town of Bad Säckingen. This was one of the first bridges built over the Rhine, sometime between 1570 and 1620. As we stop for a quick tour, you can see that the bridge and the town are still very well preserved. The bridge itself is covered and spans more than 650 feet (200 meters) across the river. A white line in the middle marks the German-Swiss border.

As we approach Basel we pass the town of Kaiseraugst. In 1982, an important discovery of Roman treasure was made at an old Roman town close to Kaiseraugst called Augusta Raurica. Although the town was abandoned hundreds of years ago, a

Above left: Bad Säckingen has one of the best-preserved wooden bridges on the Rhine. It took fifty years to build during the sixteenth century. Above: Germany, France and Switzerland meet at this precise point in the middle of the river.

smaller Roman settlement called Basilea survived. Today the town is much bigger and is known as Basel. Located across the river, Basel is our next stop.

## ✋ PEOPLE *Carnival in Basel*

The Swiss city of Basel marks an important turning point in the river. The Rhine suddenly heads north. A large post in the middle of the river marks another interesting feature of the Rhine at Basel. The post shows the exact point where the countries of France, Switzerland, and Germany meet.

Basel itself is a beautifully preserved city. It has a different character than surrounding towns and many local people even speak a dialect of German mixed in with French.

Above: By the time it reaches Basel, the River Rhine has become quite wide and can be used by larger vessels. Left: The festival of Fassnacht is a huge celebration. The colorful costumes and music here in Basel are typical of the event.

Basel is famous for its Carnival called Fassnacht. It is held for three days in the week after the Christian holiday of Ash Wednesday, which is usually toward the end of February. Throughout Europe, and in Germany in particular, festivals or carnivals are held during January and February. It is a tradition going back more than 2,000 years.

The carnivals allowed people to release their energy before the fasting period of Lent.

Basel's Fassnacht has parades, colorful costumes, public entertainment, and music. Groups of people known as *cliques* dress up in historical costumes and parade through the city streets at night with elaborate decorative lanterns to light their paths. This event is very similar to Mardi Gras festival in New Orleans.

We board one of the large industrial barges at Basel harbor for the next stage of our journey.

# 3. Controlling the Rhine

LEAVING BASEL WE ENTER a section of the Rhine that has been drastically changed by human actions. These changes have made the river flow more slowly than before and its course has been raised above the surrounding countryside. The river runs in almost a straight line along a wide valley that separates the Black Forest to the east from the French Vosges Mountains to the west. We pass the French city of Strasbourg before winding our way north to the industrial city of Mannheim and the historic city of Mainz.

Below: The ultramodern Louise Weiss building became the new home of the European parliament in 1999.

Above: The river widens to 328 feet (100 meters) near the town of Gerstheim, with France on the left and Germany on the right. Left: A border-crossing gate shows the EU flag with a warning in German and French that the gate will be closed in emergencies.

📖 HISTORY *The river as a border*

Rivers are important physical boundaries. On many maps, national borders are drawn down the middle of rivers. The Rhine forms a long-standing natural boundary between Germany and France. In this section of the river, you would speak French if you got off on the west bank, but German if you chose the east bank. In the past, battles between France and Germany have shifted the national borders. Between 1870 and 1919, for example, much of Alsace-Lorraine, the French region to the west of the Rhine, was German. After World War I, it became part of France again.

In 1979, the city of Strasbourg, 87 miles (140 kilometers) downstream of Basel, was chosen as the home of the European parliament, the governing body of the European Union (EU). This decision reflected the strong links between two of the EU's most important countries—France and Germany. France and Germany were two of the six original members of the EU. Since January 2002 the two countries, along with ten other European states, have shared the same currency—the euro.

## $ ECONOMY *Industrial heartland*

The Rhine and its tributaries flow through the industrial heartland of Western Europe, and so the river has long been a natural transportation link. Today many goods are carried by road, but the river remains an important method of transportation for large and bulky cargo, including coal, grain, timber, oil, chemicals, and iron ore. By using the river, industries can move vast amounts of material. Barges can be up to 328 feet (100 meters) long—the length of a soccer field—and hold up to 3,306 tons of grain or coal. To transport the same amount by train would require 15 large rail cars, and by road it would require at least 50 large trucks.

Transporting large amounts of goods by barge is cheaper than by rail or road. Barges also use fuel more efficiently, which is better for the environment. But the journey is slower by river, about ten times slower, so journeys must be planned well in advance to make sure that goods arrive on schedule.

## ➡ CHANGE *Rhine shipping canal*

River channels change and shift naturally. They form meanders by eroding material on one bank, where the river flows fast, and depositing it on the other, where it slows down. The bottom of the river channel also

Huge barges pass each other as they carry cargo up and down the river.

changes shape and depth because material from higher up the river is deposited where the river slows down and widens out on a level valley.

North of Basel the river's natural course has been changed to overcome the problems of sediment deposit and erosion, which change the shape and depth of the river. Because river traffic is so important to

the economy, the river has to be deep and wide enough for large ships to pass through. To form a controlled shipping canal, a channel is built between raised banks called levees. The canal actually sits a few yards above the surrounding land. The old route of the river—the *ResteRhein* MAP REF: 1 , which means "the Spare Rhine"—is below us and is now only used as an overflow channel for the main canal.

The ship canal is controlled by locks that raise and lower the level of water in the "new" channel. This ensures that there is always enough water to keep the larger boats afloat. By managing the river in this way, it is also possible to prevent flooding.

Between Rheinfelden and close to Baden-Baden, 105 miles (170 kilometers) further downstream, there are 12 enormous locks that control the waters of the Rhine.

Left: At Kembs, the channels, locks, and dams on the right highlight how humans have controlled the flow of the Rhine. The old winding river channel is on the left.
Below: After the Rhine was channelized, the old river channels have become quiet backwaters, rich in plant and animal life.

Nuclear power stations are a familiar sight on the Rhine between Basel and Strasbourg, particularly on the French side of the Rhine.

## $ ECONOMY *Nuclear power*

Nuclear power stations are a common feature along the Rhine, especially on the western, French side of the river. Nuclear power stations need large quantities of water, which the Rhine supplies, to cool down the equipment used to generate electricity. The power stations built alongside the Rhine are linked to the river by small canals. France generates 76 percent of its electricity from nuclear power—more than any other European country. In 1999, there were 19 nuclear power stations on the German side of the river, providing 30 percent of that country's electricity. They are slowly being closed down, however, as nuclear power is becoming less popular in Germany. People there are worried about the dangers from potential nuclear accidents, and have raised more successful protest against power plants than people in France have.

 NATURE *A natural treasure*

To the right of our barge are the rolling hills and forests of the Black Forest. This is one of the most scenic and popular areas of Germany. The Black Forest runs all the way from the Swiss border to the area near the cities of Karlsruhe and Stuttgart. Much of the region is covered by coniferous trees such as spruce and pine, and there are many forest trails open to walkers and bicyclists.

The Black Forest lies within the German state of Baden-Württemberg, and the state takes an active role in its conservation. Development within the forest is strictly

controlled to preserve this natural treasure for future generations.

Look out for a tall spire rising above the horizon. This is the 381-foot (116-meter) spire of the beautiful Freiburger Münster cathedral in Freiburg-im-Breisgau, the capital of the Black Forest region.

## $ ECONOMY *Clocks and cakes*

Agriculture and paper-making are important industries in the Black Forest region, but a more unusual local industry is clock-making. There is even a local tour people can take called "the Route of Clocks."

The mild climate allows farmers to grow ornamental plants, hops (for brewing), tobacco, potatoes, and grain. The Black Forest is also well known for its fine foods, many of which are exported around the world. One of its famous exports is Black Forest Cake, a delicious dessert made with chocolate, cream, and cherries.

Below: Many small tributaries flow into the river from the rolling hills of the Black Forest, which runs along the eastern bank of the Rhine.

## 🐰 NATURE *A poisonous brew*

Like many large industrial rivers, the Rhine has a long history of pollution. Since the start of the Industrial Revolution in the early 19th century, the Rhine has been used as a dumping ground for untreated waste from town sewage systems and from industries such as paper-making and chemical manufacture. In less than 200 years, the Rhine has been turned into a poisonous brew. Local species such as the Rhine salmon were completely extinct by 1940. The construction of canals, locks, and weirs has also disrupted the natural habitat, threatening any species that might have survived the pollution.

## ➡ CHANGE *Cleaning up its act?*

One of the most serious pollution incidents on the Rhine took place in 1986 when a fire at a chemical factory north of Basel released 33 tons of pesticides, chemical dyes, and fungicides into the river. As a result, river life died as far as 93 miles (150 kilometers) downstream. In 1987, following this incident, the six countries through which the Rhine flows announced a major cleanup campaign to reduce pollution. New laws control the amount of waste that is dumped into the river and regular monitoring is slowly helping to restore life in parts of the Rhine. Switzerland, Germany, and France now work together in Basel to keep the river clean.

Just across the border from Basel, in Germany, a monitoring station samples water from the river and checks its quality every six minutes, 24 hours a day. Industries that pollute the river can be traced and fined.

Salmon have now been reintroduced to the Rhine. By 1998 they had been seen as far upstream as Strasbourg—an encouraging sign that the Rhine is at last cleaning up its act.

Below: The salmon ladder is the series of small steps at the left of the photograph. Salmon swim upstream by jumping from pool to pool up the ladder, bypassing bigger obstacles in the main river channel.

Above: Heidelberg is a famous university town on a tributary of the Rhine. It has many historical buildings and is a popular tourist destination.

### 📖 HISTORY   *Bells of the Rhine*

About 31 miles (50 kilometers) north of Strasbourg, the Rhine again flows through a single country—Germany. Throughout the world, rivers are a natural point for the location of towns, and along this stretch of the Rhine we pass many of Germany's oldest towns. Several of them are famous for their ancient cathedrals. It is not uncommon to hear bells ringing as you pass through towns such as Worms, Speyer, and Mainz. The cathedral at Worms was built in 1000 C.E., it was made famous by Martin Luther, the founder of the first Protestant sect. He founded this faith in 1517 after attending a religious meeting at Worms.

At Mainz, we leave our barge and board a hydrofoil that will take us quickly through the Rhine Gorge.

# 4. Classic Rhine Country

THE NEXT STAGE OF OUR JOURNEY takes us through the classic Rhine landscape of steep-sided valleys, crowded with vineyards and dotted with historic towns. After leaving the Rhine Gorge, we approach the Ruhr, a major industrial center. The Rhine is joined here by some of its biggest tributaries. They increase the amount of water in the river, which can make it very swift running and extremely dangerous.

Below: The broad Rhine River flows through a typical valley with steep-sided hills and small picturesque towns squeezed along the riverbanks.

Above: The Rhine Gorge is a major wine-growing area. Vineyards line the steep banks above the river.

 NATURE *The Rhine Gorge*

As we travel north on our hydrofoil, the river meanders past Mainz, heading slightly west before turning north again. The river then enters the Rhine Gorge MAP REF: 1. The gorge was formed thousands of years ago when the river arrived at an area of mainly very hard volcanic rocks. The river found an area of weakness in the softer slate rocks and, over time, eroded a channel through this weaker section. This became the deep gorge surrounded by steep mountains and hills that we see today.

The Rhine Gorge is only as wide as the river that flows through it. This is because the rate at which the river cuts into the rock is far greater than the rate at which the sides erode to form a normal, V-shaped valley. We can see this very clearly as we travel north toward Bonn.

 NATURE *Rhine vines*

The valleys of the Rhine Gorge are lined with wine-producing vineyards. This area of the river is ideal for vines because the sunny, steep, south-facing slopes and well-drained soils produce conditions that are ideal for growing grapes.

In 2000 Germany was the sixth-largest wine exporter in the world. In 1997, a total of 241,916 acres (97,900 hectares) of land along the Rhine and its tributaries was used for cultivating vines. This accounts for 94 percent of the total wine-growing land in Germany. Two-thirds of the wine-growing areas in the Rhine are very small vineyards of less than 74 acres (30 hectares). Most of the wines produced are white. Because Germany is quite far north, the colder climate is better for growing white grapes. A high proportion of the German wine that is exported is of only medium quality. Many of the best wines are only found inside Germany.

## $ ECONOMY   *The tourist trail*

Our hydrofoil can travel at speeds of up to 40 miles (65 kilometers) an hour. It is possible to travel from Mainz to Cologne and back again—a distance of 186 miles (300 kilometers)—in just half a day. This fast transportation link has opened up this section of the river to large numbers of visitors. Several companies run package tours through the Rhine Gorge, stopping off for lunch or to visit a castle or vineyard on the way.

Tourism here has a long history. The first tourist steamships were in operation as far back as 1826. The largest side-wheeled paddle steamer in the world, the *Goethe,* is still in service, although it is the last one left on the German section of the Rhine.

Below: The last paddle steamer on the Rhine, the *Goethe,* has carried sightseers along the Rhine since 1826.  Right: The Lorelei Rock towers over the Rhine at St. Goarshausen. It is the most famous landmark on our journey.  Right top: The "Rhine in Flames" is a spectacular summer festival watched by more than half a million people every August.

## 📖 HISTORY   *Legend of the Lorelei*

As we wind our way around a long bend near Bingen, we enter one of the most exciting stretches of the Rhine—the Lorelei Valley. Romantic castle ruins, such as Stahleck and Fortress Schönburg near Oberwesel, tower above. At St. Goarshausen, we reach Lorelei Rock **MAP REF: 2**, one of the region's key tourist attractions. This is one of the most dangerous parts of our journey because of the shifting river currents.

The Lorelei Rock is 436 feet (133 meters) high. Legend has it that the rock was the home of a beautiful woman whose songs lured unsuspecting sailors to their deaths on the dangerous river shallows below. The Lorelei-Lied (Lorelei Song) is one of the most famous songs in Germany.

## ✋ PEOPLE   *The Rhine in Flames*

In August the spectacular Rhine in Flames festivals take place. The dramatic shows originally started in Koblenz in 1766. They

were organized by the ruling classes of the time, but they had died out by the end of the 19th century because the government had decided that the festivals were too expensive. In 1956 the festivals were started again to attract tourists to the area after the World War II.

The festivals come to life along the stretch of the river between Boppard and Bonn. In the biggest Rhine in Flames festival, six towns along this part of the river "burn" as a flotilla of 80 ships sails past. To re-create the "burnings," houses and restaurants along both banks of the Rhine place red lights in their windows and on their terraces. Giant flares are set off near the castles, churches, and historic buildings. The red glow of the flares and the heavy smoke make the fires look real. The flotilla sails for 11 miles (17 kilometers) down the Rhine. About 30,000 people watch from the ships and another 500,000 line the banks of the river.

###  NATURE *Tributaries of the Rhine*

As we speed downstream from Boppard, there are several tributaries entering the Rhine. They are larger than the ones we saw further upstream. The Main River joins the Rhine at Mainz, having started its journey more than 325 miles (524 kilometers) away near Bayreuth in eastern Germany. At Koblenz, we are joined by the Moselle River, which begins in the Vosges Mountains in France, about 320 miles (515 kilometers) to the south. Smaller but still important tributaries, such as the Lahn and the Sieg, join from the east. Many of these tributaries are carefully managed to prevent floods. A number of dams and reservoirs regulate the amount of water flowing into the Rhine.

The point at which the clear Moselle River joins the murky Rhine at Koblenz is known as the *Deutsches Eck* meaning German Corner. The two rivers are quite different in color.

### NATURE *Living with risk*

Despite efforts to control floods along the river, nature is still a powerful force, especially on a river as large as the Rhine. During periods of heavy rainfall, the tributaries increase the amount of water in the main river channel, which causes periodic flooding.

The cathedral city of Cologne and other nearby towns and agricultural areas are regularly affected. Severe flooding took

Regular flooding causes extensive damage in riverside cities such as Cologne. This picture was taken after a torrential rain in January 1995.

place in the area four times during the 1990s. The flood of 1993 was the worst ever —the river was 34.9 feet (10.63 meters) above its normal level. Five people were killed and 2,642 gallons (10,000 liters) of heating oil from homes and factories leaked into the floodwaters. In the suburb of Rodenkirchen, which was badly affected by the floods, residents finally persuaded the city government to extend flood protection to their homes. Portable flood barriers were introduced, which prevented further damage to homes during a flood in 1999.

Despite the improvements, the Rhine is still an unpredictable river, and even the best barriers might not prevent flooding in the future.

**PEOPLE** *Carnival time again*

At the end of February, there are five exciting days of busy carnival celebrations in Cologne. One of the festival days is dedicated to women who have the freedom to play pranks on men, such as cutting off men's ties.

The highlight is the last day, *Rosenmontag*. The name comes from the German word, *rasen,* which means to rave or run wild. A big procession takes place when huge carnival figures are paraded along the streets. Floats are decorated with figures celebrating historical, political, and legendary events, and there are more than 100 bands playing music. Horse-drawn carriages pass through streets crammed with hundreds of thousands of cheering people. The procession in 2002 covered 4 miles (6.5 kilometers) and lasted for many hours.

Left: These barges at Duisburg are loaded with coal, plastic, and other goods.

## ➡️ CHANGE *Inland ports*

The Rhine is the main transport waterway of Western Europe. River traffic has been toll-free since 1816. In this section of the river, between Mainz and the Ruhr, more than 1.2 billion tons of cargo are transported each year. North of Cologne, large barges and steamers carry iron ore, gasoline, oil, coal, and grain to the Ruhr and Rotterdam. We also see push barges, or tugboats, pushing up to six barges that are joined together.

Most vessels stop at the Duisport in Duisburg, the largest inland port in the world. Duisport developed when the small boats carrying coal from the Ruhr area to the east needed to find a place to transfer their cargoes onto the bigger Rhine boats. These larger boats are cheaper to run but, because of their size, they can only sail on the main river channel. Duisport harbor covers an area of 2,471 acres (1,000 hectares) and handles about 551 million tons of cargo every year.

## 💲ECONOMY *The Ruhr District*

As we pass Duisburg, to the east is one of the most important concentrations of industry in Western Europe, known as the *Ruhrgebiet,* or

Ruhr District. It is named after a tributary of the Rhine. The district first developed during the Industrial Revolution of the early 19th century at the point where the two rivers, the Rhine and the Ruhr, meet. A number of towns—Essen, Duisburg, Dortmund, and Gelsenkirchen—developed around huge iron, coal, and steel works. This urban area, known as a conurbation, has a combined population of more than 5 million people. The river barges still carry large loads of iron, coal, and steel today, proving how important the Rhine remains to the economies of the region. The Ruhr

Above: Though small, this tugboat can push six fully loaded barges in front of it.

District alone produces 31 percent of the European Union's coal and 11 percent of its steel.

The district is changing as minerals such as coal become scarce. People prefer cleaner and safer fuels and industries. New industries, such as mechanical engineering and high-tech computing, are providing new opportunities as the coal industry and other traditional industries decline.

Left: The great crested grebe is one of many bird species found in nature reserves on the river between the Ruhr District and the Netherlands.
Below: Leisure activities like sailing are popular on the Rhine.

**PEOPLE** *Enjoying the river*

Between Duisburg and the Netherlands, we pass close to the towns of Kleve and Wesel in the area known as *Unterer Niederrhein,* (meaning under lower Rhine) MAP REF: 3 in the Rhine floodplain. About 40 percent of the area is set aside as a nature reserve. It covers 61,776 acres (25,000 hectares), most of which are wetlands. This means it qualifies as a Ramsar site. Ramsar is an international agreement that recognizes and protects important wetland areas. The reserve includes several different protected areas. It is an excellent place to go bird-watching for green-winged teal, tufted duck, lapwing, golden plovers, great crested grebes, black-tailed godwits, and reed warblers.

The nature reserve includes large areas of flooded gravel pits and open riverbanks with sand and pebble shores. People take part in many recreational activities, here such as sailing, motorboating, windsurfing, fishing, swimming, and camping.

**NATURE** *Agriculture*

Some of the main crops grown in this part of the Rhine include corn, tobacco, sugar beets, and vegetables. The downside of this agricultural activity is that farmers use large amounts of fertilizer to try to increase crop

Above: The spraying of agricultural land with chemicals near rivers has serious environmental effects. Fertilizers are washed off the land and pollute the river water.

yields. Over time the fertilizers build up in the soils and plant life, and they can also run off the fields and find their way into the Rhine and other rivers. In fact, agricultural chemicals (and especially fertilizers) are the main source of pollution on the Rhine.

The water quality of the river is affected and the chemicals can harm, and even kill, fish and plants. This is because the nutrients contained in the fertilizers encourage the growth of tiny aquatic (water-based) plants called algae. If the algae grow at a faster rate than the fish living in the river can eat them, large mats of algae form on the surface of the river. This process stops the sunlight from reaching the algae underneath. Without sunlight, the algae and other aquatic plant life die and begin to rot. This process, called eutrophication, starves the water of oxygen. Without oxygen, fish and other aquatic animals die.

Today the Rhine is better protected from pollution by European Union laws on clean water. However, these laws cannot stop all pollution. Pollutants can travel great distances in groundwater or can be suddenly washed into rivers during heavy rains. This means that some fertilizers will always get into the Rhine. One solution would be for farmers to stop using agricultural chemicals by switching to organic farming.

We board a large oceangoing cargo vessel at Emmerich. We can follow the main river channel into the Rhine Delta in the Netherlands.

# 5. The Rhine Estuary

THE COURSE OF THE Rhine becomes complicated as it nears the sea. Its delta has many separate channels that run into the sea at different places along the coast. At this point the Rhine is an estuary. As we crisscross this landscape of windmills and canals, it becomes hard to figure out exactly where we are on the river. We stick to what most people consider the main channel, which passes Rotterdam and the huge Europoort before entering the North Sea.

Below: The Rhine splits into many separate channels as it enters the Netherlands. The channels are all linked by canals.

## HISTORY · *War in the Netherlands*

During World War II, the river channels in the Netherlands and northern Germany were of great military importance. As the German army was forced out of France by the Allied (American and British) Forces in 1944, fierce battles were fought to capture important bridges over the Rhine. We pass under some of these bridges as we travel past the towns of Nijmegen and Arnhem. The Germans blew up the bridges after crossing them to slow down the Allies. The Allies were in a constant race to capture the bridges before the Germans destroyed them.

## NATURE · *Dutch river channels*

In the delta region, the flow of water slows down as the Rhine reaches the flat land near the sea. As it slows, the river begins to deposit the sediment it is carrying, causing it to spread out and split into several channels. This happens to the Rhine as it reaches the Netherlands. As the river splits a number of new channels are formed, each with a different name. The main channels, through which about two-thirds of the water flows, are called the Lek and the Waal. The Lek continues west to Rotterdam and enters the North Sea at Hoek van Holland, meaning Hook of Holland. The Waal also flows west and merges with other smaller tributaries to form the Hollandschdiep, an arm of the North Sea. A third channel, known as the Crooked Rhine, leads to Utrecht and continues west to the sea as the Old Rhine.

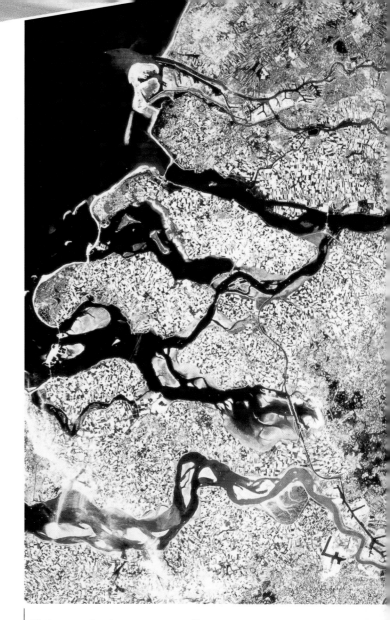

This satellite image of the Rhine estuary shows some of the channels as they reach the sea. The Lek is the channel closest to the top of the picture.

All the channels are part of the river's delta system and stretch from north of Amsterdam to as far south as Antwerp in Belgium. We will follow the Lek, which most people consider to be the main channel through the delta region.

**NATURE** *Taking on nature*

The river channels of the delta are also affected by the fact that most of the Netherlands' land is artificially low-lying. About 24 percent of the country is below sea level, which makes it very vulnerable to flooding by the sea. Much of the Rhine delta includes land that has been reclaimed from the sea over the centuries. High seawalls have been built to keep back the sea. Although the sea must be kept out to keep the land dry and the water fresh, the Rhine needs to reach the sea, too.

In the past few years, the Rhine and other rivers in the area have suffered extremely high water levels from heavy rainfall. In 1995 rivers reached unexpected heights and breached the dams, and flooding agricultural land and several towns. To avoid such problems, dams are being relocated and water meadows lowered. This allows rivers to flow more freely with fewer obstacles along their courses. The water meadows also provide a natural floodplain for excess water.

**$ ECONOMY** *Tulips from Amsterdam*

Agriculture is very important in the delta area. Flower-growing creates jobs and money for the Netherlands, which produces about 9 billion flower bulbs every year. About 7 billion of these are exported. This earned the country $4 billion in 2000.

Left: All along the Dutch coast, giant dams like this one at Afsluitdijk stop the sea from flooding the low-lying land. The sea is on the right in this picture. Below: Flower-growing, especially of tulips, is a major industry in the delta area, and every spare piece of land is used.

The most popular bulbs produced, and the ones the Netherlands is most famous for, are tulips. The Netherlands dominates world tulip production, with 80 percent of the world market. Tulips alone account for about one third of all the bulbs produced in the Netherlands. There are more than 21,078 acres of land planted with tulip bulbs. If the bulbs were planted 4 inches (10 centimeters) apart, they would circle the equator seven times.

## ✋ PEOPLE  *Land and the Dutch*

The Netherlands is one of the most densely populated countries in Europe. About 15.6 million people live in a country of just 16,033 square miles (41,526 square kilometers). In 2001 it had a population density of 959 people per square mile (375 people per square kilometer). This compares with a population density of 75 people per square mile (29 people per square kilometer) in the United States.

In their search for more land, the Dutch have been reclaiming land from the sea for 400 years. One of the biggest land-reclamation schemes started in 1932, when an inlet from the North Sea, called the Zuider Zee, was reclaimed. A dam was built to keep out the sea and the area behind the dam was drained to make new land, known as polders MAP REF: 1 . The polders provided new areas for housing and agriculture. The remaining water now forms Lake Ijsselmeer, into which drains the Ijssel, a branch of the Rhine.

Below: Amsterdam, the capital city of the Netherlands, is home to a mix of races and cultures.

### 🐰 NATURE  *Windmills*

The windmill has a strong link with the Netherlands, and it has played an important role in the development of the country. In the 17th century, windmills were used to drain the low-lying land and keep it dry and habitable. The windmills used the power of the wind to turn scoops that collected water from the marshy land. The water was tipped into large tanks and fed into rivers and small streams. By the middle of the 19th century, there were more than 10,000 windmills in the Netherlands. Today, because electrical pumps have replaced the need for wind power, only about 1,000 remain. They are a symbol of the Dutch people's close link to water and a reminder of the skills needed to build them.

However, modern windmills, known as wind turbines, are being used more and more today. The Dutch wind-energy industry is developing rapidly, mainly due to the flat, windy Dutch landscape. A single 328-foot (100-meter) wind turbine can generate up to one megawatt (MW) of electricity, enough power for up to 800 typical European households. In 2000, the Netherlands produced about 495 Megawats

Above: Along this stretch of the river we can see how wind has been used to create power by traditional (windmill on the left) and modern (wind turbines on the right) methods.

of electricity using wind turbines, which made it the seventh-largest wind producer in the world. Wind energy accounts for 1 percent of the Netherlands' total electricity supplies, compared to almost 13 percent in Denmark. But the Netherlands' share is growing fast as the Dutch seek to make more use of the flat and windy landscape. They are also developing offshore wind farms in the North Sea; they already have two such farms where the Rhine meets the sea.

### 💲 ECONOMY  *Rotterdam & Europoort*

The main channel of the Rhine River (the Lek) has been widened as it nears the sea to cope with large oceangoing vessels. As we follow this channel, it takes us to Rotterdam, the world's largest port.

Rotterdam handles industrial traffic from four of Western Europe's most important economies—the Netherlands, Germany, France, and Belgium. About 360 million tons of cargo passed through the port in

2001. That is roughly the same as one of the giant barges we've seen along the Rhine coming through the port every five minutes, every day of the year.

To cope with the huge amount of water traffic through Rotterdam, an additional port, called Europoort MAP REF: 2 was built in 1957. Europoort was built next to the North Sea, mostly on reclaimed land. It is a state-of-the-art port with the most modern equipment and storage facilities available. As we sail toward the sea, you'll be able to see the "disaster area," where firefighters are trained to deal with large-scale industrial accidents that could happen at the port. There is even a grounded tanker that is set on fire several times a day so that firefighters can practice their skills.

Below: Rotterdam is the world's largest port. It is filled with ships of all shapes and sizes.

 *Cleaning up the river*

The Rhine flows at its slowest in the delta region. As it runs out of energy, most of its sediment is deposited on the river bed. The sediment contains pollutants such as chemicals and oil that have been picked up from the many industries the river has flowed past on its journey.

As the sediment builds up, it can disrupt shipping, so the river has to be dredged regularly. The sediment is removed and dumped in other parts of the delta or in the North Sea. The city of Rotterdam alone has to dredge about 11 million tons of polluted sludge from the harbor basin every year. It was estimated during the 1980s that the Rhine contributed 40 per cent of the pollution in the North Sea.

Efforts have been made in recent years to reduce the amount of pollution in the delta area. One method has been to clean the sediment, but this is expensive. In the 1980s, it was estimated that cleaning sediment from the Dutch part of the Rhine would cost about a million dollars a year. The Dutch have since decided that it is cheaper to reduce the pollution entering the river to start with. New methods of recycling waste have been developed by industries along the river. As a result, the amount of polluted sediment has been halved.

Left: Pollution from the delta area finds its way to the sea. Algal bloom affects sealife on the Dutch coast.

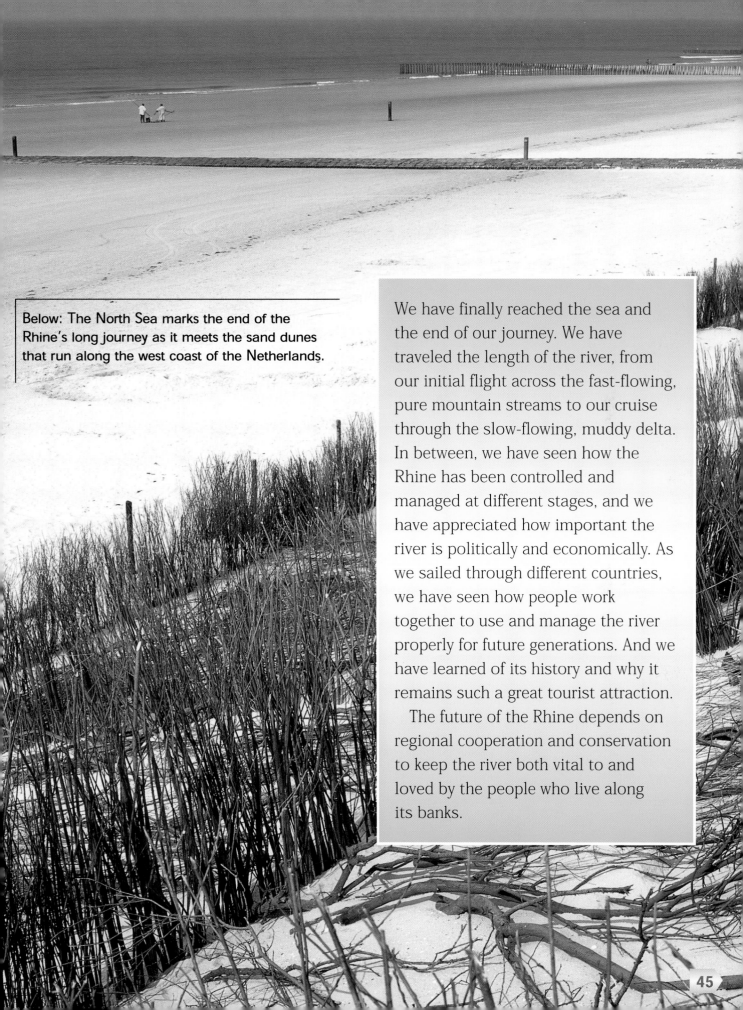

Below: The North Sea marks the end of the Rhine's long journey as it meets the sand dunes that run along the west coast of the Netherlands.

We have finally reached the sea and the end of our journey. We have traveled the length of the river, from our initial flight across the fast-flowing, pure mountain streams to our cruise through the slow-flowing, muddy delta. In between, we have seen how the Rhine has been controlled and managed at different stages, and we have appreciated how important the river is politically and economically. As we sailed through different countries, we have seen how people work together to use and manage the river properly for future generations. And we have learned of its history and why it remains such a great tourist attraction.

The future of the Rhine depends on regional cooperation and conservation to keep the river both vital to and loved by the people who live along its banks.

**From the Swiss Alps to the North Sea, the Rhine falls more than 5,900 feet (1,800 meters) on its 820 mile (1,320 kilometer) journey.**

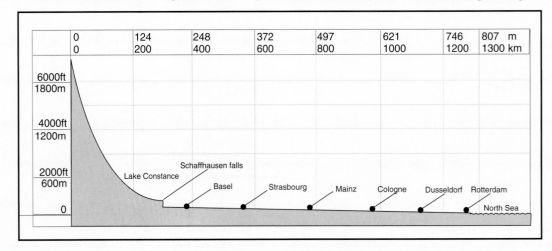

# *Further Information*

## Useful websites

www.iksr.org/icpr
The website of the international commission for the protection of the Rhine contains valuable information on pollution and other threats to the Rhine.

www.germany-info.org/relaunch/index.html
The official website of the German embassy in the United States

www.netherlands-embassy.org
The official website of the Dutch embassy in the United States

www.swissemb.org
The official website of the Swiss embassy in the United States

www.info-france-usa.org
The official website of the French embassy in the United States

## Books

Allan, Tony. *The Rhine.* Milwaukee: Gareth Stevens, Inc., 2003.

Chandler, Virginia. *The Changing Face of France.* Chicago: Raintree, 2002.

Pollard, Michael. *The Rhine.* New York: Marshall Cavendish Corporation, 1997.

Schanz, Sonja. *The Changing Face of Germany.* Chicago: Raintree, 2002.

# Glossary

**algal bloom**  algae are tiny plants that live in the sea. Occasionally the algae grow very fast, or "bloom" and make large visible patches near the surface of the water. This process can be harmful to other sea life.

**causeway**  raised path or road over marshland or water

**channelization**  creating a channel, or directing something through a channel.

**conurbation**  extended urban area made up of a number of towns that all join together

**delta**  geographical feature at the mouth of a river, formed by the buildup of sediment

**desalinisation**  making of fresh water from sea water by removing the salt

**downstream**  direction you travel along a river when you are moving from the source to the estuary

**erosion**  wearing away of land by natural forces such as running water, glaciers, wind, or waves

**estuary**  area where fresh water and salt water mix, usually found where rivers enter the sea

**eutrophication**  gradual increase in the concentration of phosphorus, nitrogen, and other plant nutrients in an aging aquatic ecosystem such as a lake

**flood**  when a river spills over its banks, onto land that is usually dry

**floodplain**  part of a river valley submerged during floods

**flotilla**  small fleet of ships or boats

**glacier**  large body of continuously accumulating ice and compacted snow, formed in mountain valleys or at the poles that deforms under its own weight and slowly moves

**gorge**  deep, narrow river valley with steep, rocky sides

**groundwater**  water that is stored or moves underground in the soil or rocks

**headwaters**  streams that make up the beginning of a river

**hydrofoil**  boat with winglike blades attached to its hull (bottom of the boat). The blades lift the boat out of the water as it increases in speed.

**landslide**  sudden, rapid movement of soil or rock down a slope

**levee**  long, narrow bank that keeps the river within its channel. Levees may be natural or artificial barriers.

**meander**  large bend in a river, usually "S" shaped

**meltwater**  water produced by the melting of snow and ice

**navigable**  passable by ship or boat. A waterway is navigable when it is deep enough and wide enough to allow ships or boats to sail through it.

**organic farming**  raising of livestock or plants without using artificial chemicals

**pesticides**  any poison, organic or inorganic, used to destroy pests of any sort

**polder**  piece of land reclaimed from the sea, usually surrounded by dams so that the water level can be artificially regulated

**reservoir**  artificial lake that forms when water collects behind a dam. Reservoir water may be used for irrigation or for producing hydroelectric power.

**salmon ladder**  series of stepped pools through which salmon can move up a river. They jump from pool to pool until they reach the top level; they can then swim normally upstream.

**sediment**  fine sand and earth that is moved and left by water, wind, or ice

**source**  point at which a river begins

**toll**  tax or charge on individuals or traffic allowing them to pass a certain point

**tributary**  stream or river that flows into another larger stream or river

**upstream**  direction you travel along a river when you are moving from the estuary back toward the source

**waterfall**  sudden fall of water over a steep drop

**water meadow**  meadow that is regularly flooded by a stream or river. Normally part of a river's floodplain.

**weir**  fence or enclosure set in a waterway for the purpose of catching fish

**wetland**  area of marsh or swamp where the soil is saturated with water like a sponge

# Index